Series 661

The authors of the Ladybird 'Words for Number' Series are authorities on the teaching of reading, and joint authors of the research work — 'Key Words to Literacy' published by The Schoolmaster Publishing Co. Ltd.

W. Murray is an experienced headmaster and lecturer, and is author of the Ladybird Key Words Reading Scheme. J. McNally, now engaged on further research work, was Chief Educational Psychologist to Manchester Education Committee.

Book I

THE LADYBIRD
WORDS FOR NUMBER SERIES

Understanding Numbers

by
J. McNALLY and W. MURRAY
(Authors of 'Key Words to Literacy')

with illustrations by
KENNETH INNS

Publishers: Ladybird Books Ltd . Loughborough
© Ladybird Books Ltd (formerly Wills & Hepworth Ltd) 1966
Printed in England

1
Number one

The boy has

one head,

one nose,

one mouth.

He has one dog.

1

one boy

2
Number two

The girl has
two eyes,
two ears,
two hands.

She has two kittens.

2 are more than
1

1 and 1 make 2

The girl has two kittens.

3
Number three

Here are three children,
three pets,
three dishes,
three baskets
and
three birds.

 3 are more than
2

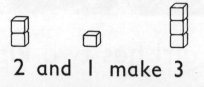

2 and 1 make 3

The three children have
three pets.

4
Number four

The dog has four legs.

The kitten has four legs.

The cat has four legs.

One child has two legs,
so two children have
four legs.

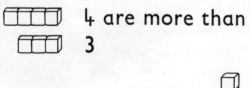 4 are more than
3

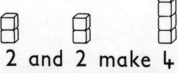
2 and 2 make 4

All the pets have four legs.

5
Number five

The girl is five. She has
five fingers on each hand
and five toes on each foot
She has five dolls
and five balls.

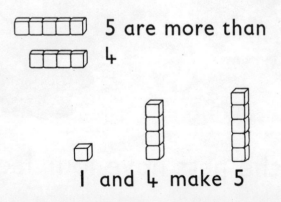

5 are more than
4

1 and 4 make 5

The girl has five dolls
and five balls.

6
Number six

The boy is six.

He has six cards.

Each card has 6 on it.

There are six candles

and six presents.

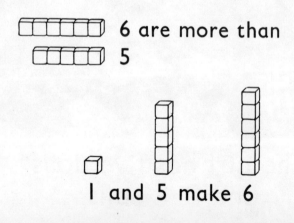

6 are more than
5

1 and 5 make 6

The boy is six years old.
He has six presents.

7
Number seven

The girl is seven.

She has seven cards.

Each card has 7 on it.

There are seven candles

and seven presents.

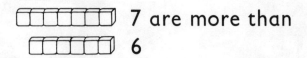 7 are more than
6

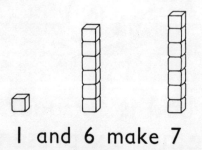

I and 6 make 7

The girl is seven years old.
She has seven presents.

8
Number eight

There are four children.

They have eight legs.

There are two dogs.

They have eight legs.

There are eight birds
and eight trees.

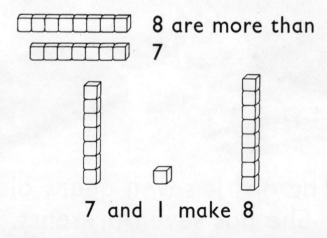

8 are more than
7

7 and 1 make 8

There are eight birds and
eight trees.

9
Number nine

There are nine children.
They have nine balloons,
on nine strings.
Three balloons are red,
three are blue and
three are green.
Three threes make nine.

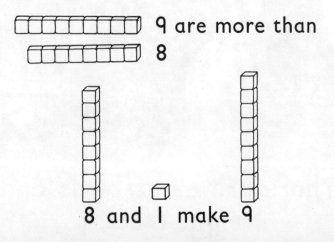

9 are more than 8

8 and 1 make 9

There are nine children
with nine balloons.

10
Number ten

The girl is ten years old.
Her two hands have
ten fingers.
Her two feet have ten toes.
There are ten plants
in ten pots.

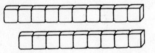 10 are more than
9

9 and 1 make 10

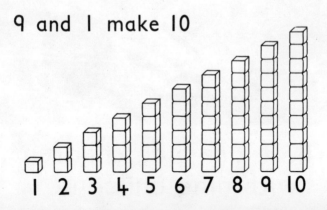

1 2 3 4 5 6 7 8 9 10

The girl is looking at
ten plants.

11
Number eleven

The boy is eleven years old.

He is going to write eleven names

of eleven boys for football.

Eleven make a football team.

A team plays eleven other boys.

11 are more than 10

10 and 1 make 11

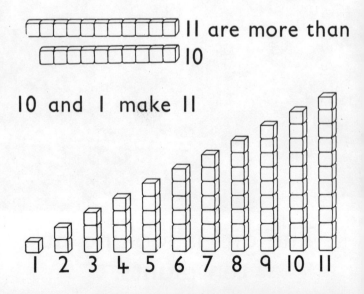

1 2 3 4 5 6 7 8 9 10 11

He is going to write
eleven names.

12
Number twelve

Here are twelve eggs. Twelve ones.
Here are twelve buns. Two sixes.
Here are twelve shoes. Six twos.
Here are twelve marbles. Four threes
Here are twelve balls. Three fours.

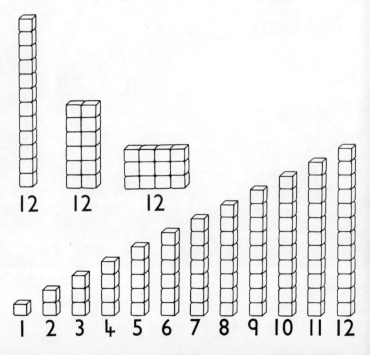

12   12   12

1 2 3 4 5 6 7 8 9 10 11 12

big   little

Here are two boys,
a big boy
and a little boy.

The big boy has
a big apple
and the little boy
has a little apple.

some   all

Here are some children.
Some have toys and
          some have no toys.

All the children have
          ice-creams.
They all like ice-cream.
All children like ice-cream.

long   short

The man has a long ladder.

The boy has a short ladder.

One balloon has a short
string.

The other has a long string.

up   down

The boy goes up.
He looks up.

The man comes down.
He looks down.

One girl's balloon goes up.
The cat jumps down.

first   last

The boy in red is first.
The boy in blue is last.

The girl is first.
She sees her name is first.

The boy is last.
He sees his name is last.

1   Jane Smith

2   Mary Brown

3   Ronald Parker

4   William Bates

5   Joan Gray

6   Charles Walker

7   Tony Soames

8   Richard Thomas

9   Jean Burton

10 Jack Owen

in   out

The dog goes in.
The cat comes out.

IN   OUT

The boy goes in.
The girl goes in.

The man comes out.
The woman comes out.

IN

OUT

new   old

(1) An old toy.
A new toy.

(2) An old hat.
A new hat.

(3) An old car.
A new car.

more

(1) The boy wants some more.
He has some more.
The girl wants some more.
She will have some more.

(2) Are there more green beads
than blue beads, or are
there more blue beads than
green beads?

(3) Are there more yellow sweets
than red sweets, or are there
more red sweets than yellow
sweets?

under   over

The bus is going over
the bridge.
The boat is going under
the bridge.

The boy goes over
the fence.
The dog goes under
the fence.
The bird is over a tree.
The horse is under a tree.

buy   shop   money

The girl has some money.

She wants to buy some
flowers.

She can buy from this shop.

The boy has some money.

He wants to buy some
apples.

He can buy apples in
this shop.

day   night   time

It is day time.
Children are at play.
The sun shines in the
day time and the
birds sing.

It is night time.
The sun has gone down.
The moon is in the sky.
At night time children
sleep.

big   little   first   last

up   down   in   out

new   old   long   short

under   over   money

shop   sun   moon

one   two   three   four   five   six

seven   eight   nine   ten   eleven   twelve